Are We Creative Yet?

Text by DuPont Employees

Cartoons by Bob Thaves

ACA
PRESS
Austin, Texas

Preface to the Second Edition
"To promote a more creative society"

Much has changed in the fifteen years since the DuPont Company's former Oz Creative Thinking Network published 20,000 copies of *Are We Creative Yet?* Nevertheless the work's timeless wisdom communicated humorously through 60 essays paired with 105 of Bob Thaves' *Frank and Ernest* cartoons, remains as useful today as it did then.

Created to communicate the basic concepts of creativity and innovation, *Are We Creative Yet?* was the result of hundreds of DuPont employees contributing brief essays that pair their personal experiences with Thaves' cartoons. In so doing, Oz Network achieved its founding purpose of building on the DuPont tradition of creativity and innovation.

The American Creativity Association is a nonprofit organization that shares a similar vision: to promote a more creative society. In republishing this work, the ACA seeks to share its fundamental wisdom with thousands of people who share our concern for promoting and applying creativity in our daily lives and in all of our society's institutions.

We are grateful to the DuPont Company and cartoonist Bob Thaves for permitting us to republish and further disseminate *Are We Creative Yet?*

David Tanner
Past Director, DuPont Center for Creativity & Innovation
Past President, American Creativity Association

&

Barry Silverberg
Executive Director, American Creativity Association
(www.amcreativityassoc.org)
Director, Center for Community-Based & Nonprofit Organizations
at Austin Community College

Are We Creative Yet?

The Funny Serious Stuff is by **Bob Thaves**

The Serious Serious Stuff is by:

Bonita Bailey	Corey Ericson	Merle Mentzer
Steve Beare	Dick Ernst	Tom Nelson
Jack Billet	Steve Gleich	Charlie Prather
Dick Blomberg	Jim Green	Jean Prideaux
Franklyn Carter	Robert Hammond	Peggy Rook
Jim Casto	Rachel Hardison	Elwood Roth
Edgar Chavez	Lee Hoffman	Mary Roush
Paul Cole	Chris Holbrook	Gayle Rulifson
Alex DeDominicis	Carol Knotts	Dave Tanner
Fred Dickson	Clarence Mahoney	Jim Webster

Why This Book?

The purpose of this book is to introduce or to reinforce those aspects of creativity which the authors believe are important to enhancing the creation and implementation of useful ideas. Though these aspects are expressed from the perspective of DuPont personnel primarily for other DuPont personnel, we hope (and believe) that much of what you see and read is applicable to fostering and enhancing creativity in other work environments and in personal situations as well.

We could have elected to present our message with words alone, but we wanted to engage the artistic (right) as well as the analytical (left) side of your brain by using drawings—and we wanted you to have some fun! We don't think we could have found a better source of visual material than the genius of Bob Thaves as expressed through his creations "Frank" and his friend "Ernest."

Incidentally, this book was designed so that each day you could glance at a cartoon and its accompanying text to "bring the message of creativity home." If you're concerned about appearances at work, we suggest you place it between your feet under you desk.

The Oz Group

Contents

Foreword
The Oz Group

This book is a project of the Oz Group, an informal group of DuPonters promoting an environment for creativity and innovation. The Oz Group was founded in March, 1986, when seven DuPonters (Corey Ericson, Jim Green, Jim Magurno, Charlie Prather, Dave Tanner, Tim Weatherill, and Nat Wyeth) met to exchange views about creativity. The Oz name was coined in a discussion with Dr. Edward deBono, our first creativity consultant, when we were metamorphically describing the nature of our group—"a creativity pick-up team on a bumpy road to a brighter future as in the *Wizard of Oz*." The Oz name stuck. Since then the Oz Group has grown to over 800 Duponters (1998) representing most DuPont departments and functions. Our vision of the ideal future state:

- Creativity and innovation are valued at all levels in the organization and management behavior consistently signals and reinforces that value.
- DuPonters are knowledgeable about the technology of creativity and innovation and are applying the skills they develop.
- DuPonters have the space and take the time to be more creative and innovative.

The genesis of the *Frank and Ernest* cartoon project, conceived by Fred Dickson, a member of Oz, is described on Page 19. For more information about the Oz Group, contact Charlie Prather, "Convenor" of the group, or Theresa Kardos, Creative Administrator of the group, through the DuPont directory.

Dave Tanner
Founder of the Oz Group

Chapter One

The Creative Environment

The Creative Environment

If creative thinking is desired as a normal way of attacking problems within an organization, then a culture that values creativity must be nurtured.

The organization's leadership must give status to creativity, and the organization's extrinsic reward and recognition system must demonstrate the valuing of creativity.

There are intrinsic ways to value creativity as well. Important among these is giving people latitude to develop their own approaches to problem solving. People for whom someone else does the thinking will not be creative at work. They need to generate their own paths, to make mistakes, to learn from them, and then ultimately chart the path to the solution.

Don't Judge Too Soon

An idea that at first seems foolish may later turn out to be the key to a quantum jump improvement.

In a problem-solving session about continuity of operation of a belt filter, it was said, "Well, we wouldn't have this problem if the filter didn't move." It seemed stupid! But that comment led to an improved process concept where there was no relative motion between the belt and the vacuum box.

Handle Newborns with Care

Soon after its birth, the infant idea is delicate and precious. It can be killed by a sneer or a yawn. It can be stabbed to death by a snicker and worried to death by a frown on another person's brow.

Accentuate the Positive

This is one of the best ways to support the creative growth of others. People who know they are supported and appreciated will be motivated to apply more of themselves to whatever the task.

If you have innovators in your organization who fail—which will happen many times—they need positive reinforcement. When was the last time you recognized and acknowledged good work or a creative idea?

Do something nice for yourself, too! Recognize your own good work! Applaud yourself, feel good, and continue to grow.

Harness the Subconscious

Even if you're trying to solve a problem by yourself, you're not alone. Learn to harness the power of your subconscious for creative problem solving. For example, you can "put aside" a difficult problem and come back to it later. You'll find that your subconscious has done a lot of the work while you were otherwise occupied.

Or, use your subconscious more directly: sit quietly, close your eyes, shut off your internal dialogue, and let your mind freely pursue the topic. The answers will come!

If You Can't Say Something Nice ...

Nothing shuts down a hot creative session faster than the inhibitions generated by the fear of ridicule. Never make a team member feel bad because he or she expressed a "dumb" idea. If an idea can't be built upon immediately, shelve it or pass it by, but don't say anything to insult its parent. It can only be detrimental to a free-wheeling discussion.

Use Ha Ha to Create Aha!

A joke can make you see an unexpected connection, and you say "Ha Ha." A creative idea makes you see an unexpected connection and you say "Aha." The processes are very similar. We use the similarity to stimulate creativity in our area by sending our colleagues a "daily joke" by electronic mail. At first, people resisted the idea, but soon they were looking forward to it and even sending us jokes to use—further fostering a fun, creative environment.

Don't Worry! Be Happy!

*It's no accident that happy, positive people tend to be the most creative.
They are the types that don't sit around and complain, but are always
looking to find a solution to the problem.*

Value People

People are the single greatest value-added resource in any business. If their talents are allowed to blossom and they are made to feel important, they will become stakeholders in the company and its business. They then have a key incentive to work harder and contribute more toward making the company a success—it's theirs.

Are We Creative Yet?

18

Genesis of *Are We Creative Yet?*

Fred Dickson, a Patent Associate, was frustrated for years by the difficulty of understanding how creative people think and of teaching others how to do it, too. But he had noticed how many *Frank and Ernest* cartoons have a creativity theme. Could these be used to add fun to a serious message?

Fred contacted Bob Thaves, the creator of *Frank and Ernest*, and found that Bob would be interested in working with the Oz Group on a book devoted to creativity.

Then, to make it a company-wide project, Alex J. Demoninics suggested that we hold a contest to find the best expressions and examples of creativity and innovation from people at all levels and of all occupations within the company. The contest and its rules were described in *DuPont Directions* magazine and it wasn't long before we had over 400 submissions originating from ten countries and twenty-five states in the U.S.

The essays selected are the ones you see in this book.

Are We Creative Yet?

Chapter Two

Setting Your Personal Stage for Creativity

Plan(t) Seeds for the Future

Working creatively is something for which plans can be made and seeds planted. Every time you expand your horizons into something new you plant the seeds of future creativity. The seeds may take some time to grow, but they will.

Mental Exercise

The way to become a good Ping-Pong player is to play Ping-Pong. The way to become a creative thinker is to spend time thinking creatively. Set aside daily some time period when your mind is likely to be clear of cobwebs. Develop a list of problems and keep a pad and pencil or tape recorder handy. Decide the day before what problem to focus on. That gets the incubation process going.

Do a little bit of creative thinking each day, and soon you will have done a great deal. And it gets easier and easier.

Thinking Is Allowed

While all of us must be prepared for flashes of insight in unfamiliar places, we each have a few places where we tend to be our most creative. Often it's in a "non-business" setting—at the beach or a mountain retreat, on the golf course or tennis court, in the car, in bed—even in the bathroom.

Use these places to your creative advantage, but also strive to create a working environment that shares some of the characteristics of your personal Inspiration Point. Change the lighting, move the furniture, forward your phone calls, close and lock the door—whatever it takes. Thinking <u>is</u> allowed!

An Open Mind

Sometimes we set out to solve one problem or invent one thing, and we wind up solving another problem or inventing something else. The key is a "prepared" or open mind. If we're so focused on the original problem, we might completely overlook what we've discovered.

Our history is full of unexpected discoveries. For example, KEVLAR was to be a tire yarn and now finds its major uses elsewhere.

KEVLAR is a registered DuPont product.

Sometimes, Do It Yourself

Teams are a key to success, but there are times when you just have to do it yourself. There have been many success stories of products championed by a committed individual who saw a value that the larger group just couldn't see.

But, if you go this route, be honest with yourself, and do your best to take many different points of view into consideration.

You Are the Final Judge

The successful creative thinker carefully weighs all options, but shouldn't necessarily take one as the final word.

When seeking advice, they must recognize the dull skeptic, esteem the pure prophet, listen to the visionary, value the experienced, suffer with the fearful, praise the hopeful, thank the helpful—and then go where their own best judgment dictates.

Enthusiasm Spreads

At the end of a play or concert, a single person standing, applauding and yelling "Encore!" can get the rest of the audience on their feet and shouting. It's the same in creative problem solving. One person on fire can spread that zeal to others, and help create a committed, enthusiastic team that won't give up until the problem is solved.

Take the Plunge!

Sometimes the most difficult part of attacking a problem is getting started. A need to dot all the i's and cross all the t's can lead to abandoning our problem-solving efforts before we begin. Just take the plunge and immerse yourself in a problem. New slants and approaches will suggest themselves.

And, the positive feeling associated with overcoming the inertia of "getting ready to get ready" can be a source of energy for continuing the effort.

Create a Crisis

For some people creative ideas often come faster as a deadline approaches. They need a crisis to stimulate creativity.

Would setting deadlines for yourself help stimulate your creative talents?

Opportunities in Deviations

Don't look at deviations from the norm as just problems, but as potential opportunities.

For example, if you look at a curved flashlight beam as a problem, you'll "solve" it by buying new batteries. If you look at it as an opportunity, you may get rich marketing a flashlight that shines around corners.

Technology Push or Market Pull?

Which comes first—market need or the technology?

Some say you need to identify the need and then develop the technology. That's right!

Others say that if you have some unique technology, then you need to push it into the market place. That's right, too!

If we didn't pay attention to market need, we would too often develop technology no one wanted. But if we didn't pay attention to our technology and continue to refine it and to push it, then we would never have developed the transistor, or the laser, or the photocopier.

Capture Your Ideas

When are you your most creative? At bedtime? When you wake up? When jogging? In the shower?

Whenever the ideas flow, don't lose them! Keep a notebook by the bed, or in the bathroom, or put a tape recorder in your car. Do whatever's best for you.

Take a Break

We can let the pressure of meeting a deadline negatively affect our thinking process. Our minds become boggled and chained, resulting in cloudy thoughts and false perceptions. If you find yourself facing a similar situation, it's time to take a break.

Your mind is far more powerful when it has the opportunity to cogitate in a relaxed state. Take a nap if you like. But if you do this on the job, make sure you have a brilliant idea ready prior to being awakened by your boss.

Break Your Mental Chains

Watch the birds in the sky rise and soar, dive and turn, and go where they want without restriction. There are no sidewalks up there—no trails to limit their flight.

But, our minds are restrained with halters and bindings. Habit and discipline have limited them to often-traveled streets. Set free, they will go like the birds to where they have never gone before. Who can say what we then will know?

Characteristics of the Creative Thinker

- Has an absolute discontent with the status quo; stirs things up.

- Is never satisfied with the first solution to a problem; seeks better alternatives.

- Explores people, places, and things outside own environment for leads to something new.

- Has a constructive attitude in problem solving; turns a negative into a positive.

- Knows when they have a good idea and "warriors" for it.

- Works hard; has an intense interest in what they are doing.

Are We Creative Yet?

Chapter Three

Overcoming Barriers

Fear
Failure
Tradition
Bureaucracy

Expose Your Idea

A significant block to creativity is fear—of being wrong, different, or of being alone with a new idea. Fear makes us delay exposure and evaluation of a creative thought. A way to overcome the "fear barrier" is to establish personal goals and a timetable.

Few ideas are perfect. But one path to improvement is to make the idea public so that others can evaluate and contribute to it. With a new idea, perfection is less important than timeliness.

Fear of Success

Yes, there are people who fear success, but more commonly we fear failure or simply making mistakes. Being innovative and making mistakes are nearly synonymous. The successful innovator will make mistakes early and cheaply, and use them as a springboard for greater success.

As a matter of fact, some believe that we learn only from our mistakes. So put your ego aside and take that risk. You might have a bumpy road along the way, but once your ideas arrive—how sweet it is!

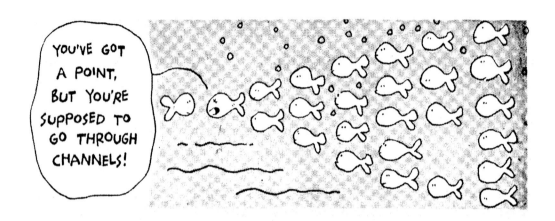

Bureaucracy Busting

Oh how stifling traditional ways can be!! Innovative ideas are often lost because they would violate some existing procedure. A creative person is a "bureaucracy buster" who does not allow tradition or form to stand in the way of progress!

Look for a tradition to push aside and experience how refreshing it can be.

Leadership

The last thing a leader of innovative people wants is to be followed by a herd. That leader should expect and demand "mavericks," "troublemakers," "bureaucracy busters."

The leader needs people who will constructively challenge the direction in which a company is headed and the standard ways of getting there.

Selling the Idea

When you have an idea, but expect some resistance to it, just having the idea may not be enough. You may first need to demonstrate its feasibility. This will frequently require that the inventor allocate time to "bootleg" the project until you demonstrate to skeptics that the idea has merit.

Bootlegging takes time, resources, and priority over something else you are expected to do. But it's much easier to get support for a new idea once it has a successful demonstration behind it.

Evolutionary Change Is Valuable, Too

Large organizations have immune systems that tend to neutralize anything that threatens to make changes too quickly. They want to hold on to the good things of the past, but recognize that they must move forward toward the future. One solution to this paradox is for business to set up a forum where new ideas are discussed and evaluated for possible implementation.

Also recognize that you can nurture your pet idea on your own. Any insightful manager will look the other way as long as your interest doesn't interfere with your current responsibilities.

Failure Is Just a Temporary Setback

Sometimes even the best ideas don't catch on because of a poor result somewhere in the middle of testing. We know the idea is still good, but can lose heart because of the temporary setback. This is the time to reflect on the cause of failure, and resolve to tackle the problem until it yields.

The Wright brothers expected setbacks as they proceeded to prove that they could take off and land a machine-powered glider. They saw each of their nearly two hundred "failures" as another step toward their goal.

If you know in your heart that your idea is sound, then press on and take flight over the heads of the less-inspired quitters.

Turn Failures into Successes—Think Positively!

People who succeed despite failures are those who are not afraid to fail. They expect some failures, analyze their failures, and turn them into successes.

Be a Troublemaker

A prominent characteristic of creative thinkers is discontentment with the status quo. They don't accept the way things are. They want to change things.

Some organizations call these people "troublemakers." But, if we are to out-think and out-perform our competitors, we need more "troublemakers" in our company.

Are We Creative Yet?

Managing a Creative Environment

To promote an environment for creative thinking, we have found the following to be pertinent:

- Be willing to give subordinates elbow room.
- Accept that subordinates will sometimes try half-baked ideas.
- Be a willing and constructive listener.
- Dwell on success rather than mistakes.
- Recognize milestones.
- Be enthusiastic, committed, and hard-working.

Are We Creative Yet?

Chapter Four

Taking Advantage of

Variety
Diversity
Perspective
Individuality

Variety in Thinking Styles

Some people prefer divergent thinking; others prefer convergent thinking. Some people come alive in the world of ideas and possibilities; others do best in the worlds of analysis and implementation. Some people think in pictures; others, in words, or in numbers.

No style is better, just different. And differences can make powerful allies. If fully tapped and utilized, these differences can increase energy, creativity, productivity, and success.

From Diversity Comes Creativity

If a team is composed only of analytical people, it's likely that only analytical solutions will be considered. If a team is composed only of conceptual people, it's likely that only conceptual solutions will be considered. If a team is composed only of engineers, there is a high probability that only engineering solutions will be considered.

A good team needs to be thoughtfully designed to include a mixture of skills and thinking modes. Be sure that people representing a variety of disciplines, as well as both left- and right-brain thinkers, are included.

View It from Another Angle

Our own ability to consider certain solutions is often limited by the "mental modes" we carry around in our heads. It's amazing how often we can find a solution to our problem "staring us right in the face" once we consciously change our viewpoint.

So You're an Expert!

You may like to think you're an expert in your field, or even a number of fields—and you well may be. But no matter how good your ideas are, there is always room for a more diverse view.

Get input from colleagues in your area, and from those with other areas of expertise. The more different ways of thinking that can be brought to bear, the greater the chance for the development of new and inventive solutions.

Don't Overlook the "Loner"

In forming any team to solve problems, remember that some of the most innovative solutions come from "lone-wolf" types. Team synergy can do some things best; but often, invention is the product of a single mind.

The Importance of Gender

Some say that males are more "left-brained" and females more "right-brained." Problem-solving sessions are often more productive when there are male and female participants, possibly because of left-brain and right-brain preferences.

But, whatever the reason, try to include both sexes in your problem-solving sessions.

Problem Solve as a Chorus Sings

If your bass singer is missing, then you can't make good music. The same is true in creative problem solving. When putting together a team it's often useful to include people not directly involved with the problem. They don't have the same mental blocks as the people who have been working on it and are familiar with it.

It can even be more valuable if those fresh eyes belong to non-technical "liberal-arts" types. Their unfamiliarity with the technical problem can lead to suggestions of new ways of doing things, and help pull you out of a technical rut.

Put Yourself in the Customer's Shoes

A great invention doesn't become a great product until someone buys it, so understanding and fulfilling customer needs is absolutely essential to success.

Winners continuously search for innovative ways to serve customers better than the competition. They ask themselves, "What does the customer really value?" and then build their daily efforts around their answers.

Get the Big Picture

We can think about things in a very detailed fashion, ore we can take an overview—a view from 20,000 feet. In creative problem solving, you need to do both. The commandments are the 20,000-foot view, and the government guidelines are the detailed map.

Get the big picture before you jump in and start solving the first problem you see.

Play the Artist

Artists see things differently. But, they weren't born that way. They work at it. They practice looking at things in more than one way.

We should be like artists when solving problems. If we accept the first adequate solution, we might deny our creative ability to find a better solution form a different perspective.

Draw Pictures

Sometimes a simple illustration can clear up the confusion caused by a language overload.

In a recent meeting, we were discussing improvements to one of our administrative systems, and the proposals got increasingly complicated. But, with a few strokes of the pen, a group member drew a quick chart. It was then easy for us to "picture" where we stood, and work on fine-tuning our ideas.

Value Diverse Experience

People are a collection of diverse personal and professional experiences, and we shouldn't underestimate the value of those experiences. They can be critical toward accomplishing your goals.

And, never diminish the value of your own experience. Be proud of it and tell others about it. You'll be surprised at how much they appreciate the gift you're sharing.

Simple Solutions to Complex Problems

The team approach to problem solving and communication will often lead to a simple solution to what might at first appear to be a complicated problem. Each member (including customer and supplier) is like the piece of a puzzle working together with all the other pieces to better understand the situation.

What looked like a "mess" can then become a success.

Are We Creative Yet?

A Word from Bob Thaves

As one engaged in daily creative endeavor, the topic of *Are We Creative Yet?* is especially meaningful to me. I appreciate the chance to be a part of this endeavor, and I am happy to see *Frank and Ernest* wedded to the words of the DuPont people.

Bob Thaves

Chapter Five

Creative Ways to Creative Problem Solving

Creative-Thinking Skills

We spend a lot of time and money developing employee expertise in engineering, or manufacturing, or marketing, but we often assume that employees' thinking skills are fully developed. That is, you either have them or you don't. You're either creative or you're not. In fact, there are about a dozen major categories of creative-thinking skills, and most individuals know how to use only a few.

In this cartoon, Frank is trying to visualize a result by using a model which approximates his portrait on a postage stamp. He's thinking with "visualization" and "modeling."

We might innovate more often if we used all of the thinking skills which could be placed at our command with some training.

Break the Rules

In many areas, breaking the rules can get you into trouble. In problem solving, it can lead you to success. When all else fails, go outside the lines that are confining the possible solutions—they're probably artificial anyway. Redefine the problem, and be receptive to the most outlandish ideas and try to build upon them.

Throw that mental rule book away!

Try a Metaphor

In problem solving, we are often hindered by boundaries we're not even aware of. A useful technique to help recognize and remove these barriers is to create a metaphor. Then, "solve" the metaphor's problem and see if any of these solutions apply to the original problem. This works because you won't have the same barriers around the metaphor.

We used this technique recently to find solutions to a problem whereby we had two major projects but enough personnel for only one of them. We created a metaphor of an airline with eight planes and only four pilots and thought of solutions for that problem. We then found several new solutions that helped us solve our original problem.

A Different Perspective

If you keep on doing what you've always been doing, you'll keep on getting what you've always been getting.

Try reversing the problem—looking at it from the opposite point of view— and see where that leads. Think it through from the point of view of the supplier rather than the customer, or as a product-based situation rather than a process-based one.

Try a Random Walk

The next time you find your thinking bogged down, leave your regular work area and go to any area with a collection of books. Pick a book at random and turn to any page. Scan it, looking for any fact, any tidbit that will spark your imagination into new territory.

If you get nothing at first, try a different page, or a different book, or a different place.

This technique can lead to solo brainstorming at its finest.

Reinvent the Wheel

Maybe it is time to reinvent the wheel. Or, at least er-examine its concept. Old literature, expired patents, or old research reports can give "renewed" insight into a problem. Importantly, they may show paths that need exploring and many that should go untrodden.

Past studies that did not end up as processes or a product may have value if something new is added. Or, what may not have been good in the past may be great today in a changed environment.

New Uses for Old Things

Many times the answer to a problem lies not in inventing something new, but finding an innovative use for something already in existence. If you see something in use elsewhere, ask yourself if you can use it in your business.

Conversely, if there is some method or process that you find helpful, think of ways your colleagues can benefit from it. One good idea can often be applied to a number of problems.

Combine Concepts

As a teenager, I spent three summers driving a combine on a wheat harvest. Today, in the creative aspects of my research, I'm still driving a combine. Many of the things I do are "combines" of other concepts and technologies that had not been brought together in just the right manner before. The individual concepts are not new, just combined in a way to give new ones.

Importance of Teamwork

Successful problem solvers know that what's important is to get the problem solved, not necessarily to get it solved solo. When you've come to a mental dead end and need a better road map, leave your ego at a rest stop and ask others for help in navigating.

Organize a team-creativity session based on brainstorming, synectics, or other techniques. It's fun and mentally challenging. You'll be riding in the passing lane in no time!

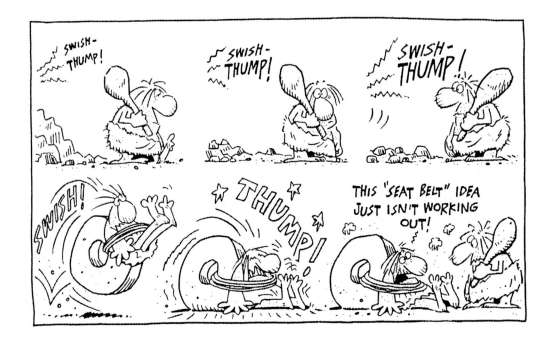

Observe Firsthand

There is no substitute for firsthand observation. By being there and "rubbing your nose in it," you get an appreciation that can't be achieved any other way. The combined simultaneous input from all five of your senses can provide a unique experience.

My daughter kept telling me that her car was driving "differently." When I finally drove it myself, it became apparent that the water pump was failing. I could hear it, feel it, and smell it. If I had depended on secondhand data, the problem could have become worse.

Hands-On Breeds Success

Sure, it's valuable to have advanced academic degrees, but the solution to a problem, even in an area in which you are expert, is often discovered by the person most closely involved with a process or procedure. "Hands-on" people can offer firsthand observations which can help improve a long-established procedure, find a more productive way to complete a task, or even start a brand-new business venture.

How observant are you?

Are We Creative Yet?

Promoting a Creative Society

For more than a decade, the American Creativity Association has been a primary resource for learning and applying creativity, innovation, problem-solving, and ideation theory, tools, and techniques. We offer a global network of creative professionals in disciplines ranging from business and industry, education, the arts, government, and nonprofit sectors. Our collective expertise provides a wide range of problem-solving methods, from simple idea-capture techniques to complex problem-solving methodologies. Above all, ACA members enjoy and benefit from personal interaction with their colleagues—top experts in the fields of creativity and innovation worldwide.

If you would like more information on the American Creativity Association, visit our website at **www.amcreativityassoc.org**.

Darlene Boyd, President (2005 - 2006)

Barry Silverberg, Executive Director - barry@amcreativityassoc.org

Are We Creative Yet?

Chapter Six

Innovation, Applying Your Creative Ideas

Work Together

The execution of an idea, like the creation of a fine tapestry, is the result of people representing a number of functions working together in a complementary fashion. If each functional representative does not fulfill his role, a quality tapestry will never be completed in time to beat the competition to the punch.

Paralysis by Analysis

Many of us have been trained to believe that there is only one right answer—and to fear giving the wrong one. As a result, we often feel that our hands are tied until we have gathered <u>every</u> detail—even those with little practical significance. And, so we sit there analyzing while a competitor seizes the opportunity.

One way to overcome this fear is to realize that implementation is not an all-or-nothing proposition. You can always "test market" an idea or product—send up a trial balloon and fine-tune on the fly.

An innovative person knows when to move from analysis to implementation, overcomes the fear—and takes action.

Fit the Peg to the Hole

Creativity can be thought of as developing the ideas, and innovation as doing something with them. Sometimes the most creative people are not the best implementers. Sometimes the best implementers are not the most creative people. Both types are invaluable.

In order to achieve your best, it is important to know at what point to get each involved in the project.

Run the Chicken Test

Sometimes an idea that looks great on paper won't work as expected in the real world. Take the example of a major aircraft manufacturer who invested heavily in a new type of jet engine. One of the mandatory capabilities of this type of component is to ingest birds in flight and continue operating. Just before commercialization, the engineers threw chickens from the grocery store into the intake—it self-destructed.

The best way to avoid wasting resources is to decide what "chicken test" your solution or development <u>must pass</u>, and find a way to run it <u>early</u>.

Start Small, Then Build

Sometimes we have to keep a low profile and start small with our creative ideas.

We wanted to do something about creativity and innovation at our plant and we spent a good deal of time talking about what we could do. It seemed like there were barriers everywhere we looked. So, we decided to start small—after all, what could it hurt? So, my office became the "Office of Innovation," and my job was redefined from secretary to "Director of the Office of Innovation," and we were in business.

Our strategy was to beg for forgiveness if we were challenged, but no one has challenged us so far.

Are We Creative Yet?

About the Funny/Serious Author

Bob Thaves began drawing cartoons as a boy in Burt, Iowa, where his father published a newspaper. As a University of Minnesota student his cartoons appeared regulary in campus newspapers and student humor magazines. The University of Minnesota later awarded Thaves an M.A. in psychology.

In 1972, while a corporate consultant in industrial psychology, Thaves created *Frank and Ernest*, and worked both careers simultaneously. The cartoon strip eventually eclipsed Thaves' other enterprises. Today *Frank and Ernest* is distributed to more than 1,200 newspapers around the world.

Bob Thaves has repeatedly won accolades from his peers. In 1984, 1985, and 1987, *Frank and Ernest* won the coveted Reuben Award for Best Syndicated Panel. In 1985, the Free Press Association honored him with the Mencken Award for Best Cartoon.

Katie and Bob Thaves live in Manhattan Beach, California. They have two children, Sara and Tom.

About the Serious/Serious Authors

The serious/serious authors began writing about creativity on the day they decided to enter the Oz Group's *Frank and Ernest* cartoon contest. They are all current or retired DuPonters or people who would like to be (that is, retired). Their backgrounds vary as do their jobs. Some are technical. Some are male. Some are female. Some are married. Collectively they live mostly in the Eastern USA and have 81 children. ... Agnes, Arthur, Blake, Charles, David, Gale, Helen, ...

Are We Creative Yet?

136

Essay Contributors

Jim Ahles   Jim Casto   Jim Green   David Martin   Mary Roush

Jean Allchin   Edgar Chavez   Mike Guschke   Keith Matlock   Ross Roussel

Walt Andrews   Jill Ciccone   Michael Harmon   Bill McCollister   Gayle Rulifson

Kay Annand   Paul Cole   Robert Hammond   David McKee   Josephine Sarro

Steven Artz   Henry Collins   Rachel Hardison   Merle Mentzer   Barbara Seningen

Mary Badger   George Connors   David Harriss   Eugene Miller   Jeff Shawd

Bonita Bailey   Sidney Cox   John Hartzler   Tom Nelson   Greg Siegel

Marvin Bailey   Harry Cress   William Harvey   Robert Newell   Robert Siegel

Roger Baker   Nils Dailey   John Hegarty   Mike O'Neill   Henry Snelling

Steve Beare   Alex DeDominicis   Lee Hoffman   Ronald Nicholas   John Stark

Jack Billet   Dan De La Cruz   Christopher Holbrook   Parry Norling   Christina Steppi

Matthew Blango   Fred Dickson   Richard Holmes   Susan Palmer   Robert Straub

Brian Blanks   Joseph Dilts   Manuel Jocson   Bob Perry   Richard Stromberg

Dick Blomberg   Charles Ellis   Barbara Jezi   Frank Pfohl   George Sutton

Chester Bloomer   Corey Ericson   Theresa Kardos   Linda Phillips   Lin Sutton

Wingard Bookhart   Dick Ernst   Vernon King   Richard Platts   Steve Waller

James Bowers   David Fisher   Charles Kirby   Charlie Prather   Dave Tanner

Edith Brady   Patrick Fitzgerald   Sharon Klahn   Jean Prideaux   James Tofsted

Ted Breuninger   Tom Gallo   Carol Knotts   Brenda Redmond   Dorothy Toto

Murray Brockman   Donald Gauger   Susan Kunkel   Jelinda Rieher   Mike Wolstencroft

Ted Brown   William Gerow   Ken Kutchek   Karen Rittenbach   Thomas Watson

Dave Burbank   Joel Gilliland   Jim Landmann   Jay Robinson   James Webster

Lee Burke   Bonnie Glassberg   Angela Lapallo   Frank Roller   Walter White

Jeff Callahan   Steve Gleich   Carlos Lores   James Romine   Gordon Whiteside

Kit Carson   Sidney Gonzales   David Lotz   Peggy Rook   Robert Writer

Franklin Carter   Michael Gordon   Art Lulay   Robert Ross III   Ginny Youngblood

Francis Casey   Theodore Grafton   Clarence Mahoney   Elwood Roth   Tony Zatkulak

Editor: Ales DeDominicis

Editing, Production, and Marketing (first edition): Edith Brady, Fred Dickson, Jim Green, Theresa Kardos, Marty Sennett, Dave Tanner

Special Acknowledgement: Steve Beare, Jean Prideaux, Jeff Shawd, Jim Howett

Editing, Production, and Marketing (second edition): Barbara Foley, Brad Fregger, Barry Silverberg

Back Cover Mind Map: Marilyn Martin - for 2005 ACA International Conference

Ordering Additional Copies of *Are We Creative Yet?*

Mail to: ACA Press
            c/o ACC CCBNO
            5930 Middle Fiskville Rd.
            Austin, TX 78752
            Attn: Circulation Editor
            512-223-7076
            www.acapress.org
            sales@acapress.org

Copies: 1-5, $20.95 each
            6-10, $19.00 each
            10-50, $17.00 each
            50-100, $15.00 each

For quantities above 100, call Circulation Editor at 512-223-7076.
Shipping (UPS Ground) and handling included in the price for quantities of
6 and above. Shipping and Handling for quantities of 1-6 is $5.00

Qualified retailers will receive a 40% discount on quantities of 10 or more.
Retailers will be charged the actual shipping cost for all quantities.

Members of the American Creativity Association receive a 10% discount on
all single-copy purchases

_____

The proceeds from this book will be used to further the activities of the
American Creativity Association's projects and programs aimed at fostering
creativity and innovation throughout the world community.

Printed in the United States
36988LVS00004BB/199-336